Countries of the Body

Praise for *Countries of the Body*

The language of Tishani Doshi's haunting, assured, delicately crafted poems, which look both east and west, is wonderfully fresh and precise.

– Ruth Padel

Tishani Doshi in her *Countries of the Body* has written some rich poems with powerful images. They have the slow curved rhythms of a dancer in their movement. The poet has a passionate sense of the sacred. Poems for her are not statements; they are meditations.... There is magic in her poems.

– U.R. Ananthamurthy

The poised yet unpredictable poems in Tishani Doshi's *Countries of the Body* are hunting for 'treasure in the dust' – streaks the mind is the stubborn progress of innocence: which 'knows nothing – little kernel of snail– /except to unfurl along his silver trail'.

– Mick Imlah

Tishani Doshi's poems have both heart and intelligence. They are rich in mysterious images, and narratives both explicit and implied. You could read them a hundred times and still find something you hadn't noticed before.

– Louis De Bernieres

Countries of the Body

Tishani Doshi

HarperCollins *Publishers* India

This edition published in India by
HarperCollins *Publishers* in 2020

HarperCollins *Publishers* India, Cyber City, Building 10-A, Gurugram,
Haryana – 122002, India
www.harpercollins.co.in

2 4 6 8 10 9 7 5 3

First Published by Aark Arts 2006

P-ISBN: 978-93-5357-622-6
E-ISBN: 978-93-5357-623-3

Typeset in 11/15 Goudy Old Style at
Manipal Technologies Limited, Manipal

Printed and bound at
Repro India Ltd.

MIX
Paper from
responsible sources
FSC® C047271

This book is produced from independently certified FSC® paper to ensure responsible forest management.

HarperCollins *Publishers*, Macken House, 39/40 Mayor Street Upper,
Dublin 1, D01 C9W8, Ireland

for Chandralekha
who helped find my body

How is it with this love,
I see your world and not you?
– Rumi

Contents

The Day We Went to the Sea

The day we went to the sea
mothers in Madras were mining
the Marina for missing children.
Thatch flew in the sky, prisoners
ran free, houses danced like danger
in the wind. I saw a woman hold
the tattered edge of the world
in her hand, look past the temple
which was still standing, as she was –
miraculously whole in the debris of gaudy
south Indian sun. When she moved
her other hand across her brow,
in a single arcing sweep of grace,
it was as if she alone could alter things,
bring us to the wordless safety of our beds.

What the Body Knows

The body dances in a darkened room
turning itself inside out
so that skin can face the light in fractures,
slip like shadow through skeleton walls,
begin to cry – really – to scream
about the tarnished weight of dreams.

This has been a drift after all.
The body returns to its original place,
moves from one to the other – creeps –
tries to flee itself, lone trunk,
searches for remain of bark,
hints of what it used to be.

Perhaps an ocean framed in bone,
a pair of birds in early white,
flying from this dream to the next
fixing the gaps between memory
and reverberation; binding spine
on vein, feather to lesion.
The body collects its wandering parts,
leans back through layers
of thickening water; roots above
boughs beneath, feet caving in to wonder.
It's how the world reverses itself,
how the distant sky finds the earth.

Undertow

I.

I hold my husband in plastic bags.
He's whispering like a soft, worn thing,
Drop me here, drop me gently.

Everything is terribly light – incense,
ash, the thinness of his voice falling
into waves, disappearing.

II.

The sea picks up my life,
empties it across itself.
I see it spilling over, dissolving.
Here are the forgotten parts –
a pink night sky, broken bangles,
a fisherman walking away from the light.

There you are, held up with wind and sails.
If you would turn, you would hear me say,
Come back, my arms ache from all the carrying.
Underneath, you're lost in a place
where everything is scraped together
and nothing is thrown back.

You sink. Colours dissolve.
You move hair from your forehead,
salt from your eyes. You're left with greys –
calling out to me, bubbles
instead of words. It is a silent death:
one I feel before it happens.

III.

Was there a child then? The child I could not have?
With hair that shakes and shines as though a sun
were gleaming under her roots. I want to stroke her.

Lean over and touch her. *Come here, let me hold you.*
I want only daughters – a thick rope of black
around her neck. She calls; the beginning of your name.

If I were really a mother, I would do it quick
and painless, out of love. Take the hair –
twist, yank, drop; tilt her over like a bag of sand.

It would be done then. There would be less
to clean up. She will never be like me.
The death of her child will kill her.

IV.

If you must collect pictures, take them
when I'm looking away. Here's a beach again –
the nets spread on the sand drying,
a fish in the corner slapping its tail.

Nothing matters then.
We'll meet when we're warm and dry.
Take this picture – my shoulders, the bone,
the shine, the criss-cross of white straps.

V.

I'm eight-years-old, running into the sea.
Run in, my mother says, *Go on then like a naked girl.*
Nobody cares, nobody's watching.

The sea pulls me in around the ankles,
grabs the sand from underneath, shows me
a glimpse of my life, what it will be like later.

It was all calm once, long ago, a teardrop
between apartment buildings. But here in my life;
Hiss hiss. This one is no good.

This one doesn't love you.
This one doesn't know what you need.
Leave, let go, stop.

The frothy fingers at my throat,
the voice pouring into me,
a terrace of vanishing blue.

You will leave this one.
You will leave this place.
For a while you will know nothing.

The Affair

These days men on curbs are curved
like farm tools or bits of wire,
like unruly saucers of tea flung
into the trees, the walls, the breeze.

Houses are shifting too –
up and going on emerald shoes,
colliding on streets, spitting
bits of brick and splinter on our sleeves.

This one holds a wife
standing at the bleak stairway of a dream,
grappling with her wedding veil;
with mothballs and pearls and girls.

See, the husband is rising – a shipwreck
disappearing against a photograph
of beaten love. He's separating pink
from dark, fodder from cloud,

movement from half-movement.
We can throw away these things:
the sweat, the chests, the hair,
the dead weight of despair dropping

into the living rooms of our lives;
the broken furniture, the cracked foundations.
I claim you back, the wife says to him.
She claims him back.

But what of this youngest one
inching along the sinew of the floor?
He knows nothing – little kernel of snail –
except to unfurl along his silver trail.

The Affair II

The Son

In a moment the boy will enter again –
a deserted city with marble eyes,
to roll his father between his fingers,
pat his chest as if it were still smooth-skinned and thin.

The boy stands in the horizon
where the sun is lowering herself in palm fronds
and jasmine garlands. She's lowering her nubile waist
into the lap of Colombo's sea.

Underneath, youth hides the bones,
the strings, the tendons,
those strained, drained depositories of manhood
ground into pelvises and hips.

Underneath, ships of worn stubble
are scraping against the beginnings of thighs, of light.
The boy exchanges bodies with his father,
watches the years change us by touch.

In a moment we become what we were.
The boy looks up from parting waters,
he throws us down like a ring of beaten flowers
tired from holding their breath.

The Father

I think he must confuse things.
Say he's moving his unbroken fingers.
Say he thinks what he's doing is stroking
his son's hair, his own hair.

He moves in straight lines
like his father and his father and the one before.
He meets himself at the door
when he sees the boy every morning.

He feels the coarse undergrowth of my hair –
its terrifying darkness. He loses continuity,
moves back and forth, around and around,
relearns how he was taught to move at birth.

His body ruptures in empty hotel rooms,
languishes with all the parts he cannot touch,
speaks with old inconsistencies,
with secrets strapped to his mouth.

We pretend we have found a place
to be this and that: created, destroyed
and maintained – a universe intact.
It is pointless then –

the boy appearing in such a way,
emerging from the sullen belly of the ocean.
I am the light of the world, he says,
as if it could change anything.

The Deliverer

OUR LADY OF THE LIGHT CONVENT, KERALA

The sister here is telling my mother
how she came to collect children
because they were crippled or dark or girls.

Found naked in the streets,
covered in garbage, stuffed in bags,
abandoned at their doorstep.

One of them was dug up by a dog,
thinking the head barely poking above the ground
was bone or wood, something to chew.

This is the one my mother will bring.

MILWAUKEE AIRPORT, USA

The parents wait at the gates.
They are American so they know about ceremony
and tradition, about doing things right.

They haven't seen or touched her yet.
don't know of her fetish for plucking hair off hands,
or how her mother tried to bury her.

But they are crying.
We couldn't stop crying, my mother said,
feeling the strangeness of her empty arms.

*

This girl grows up on video tapes,
sees how she's passed from woman
to woman. She returns to twilight corners,

to the day of her birth.
How it happens in some desolate hut
outside village boundaries

where mothers go to squeeze out life,
watch body slither out from body,

feel for penis or no penis,
toss the baby to the heap of others,

trudge home to lie down for their men again.

Later

Remember, the winds are not in your hands,
Remember, you cannot say I'll winnow, I'll winnow tomorrow.
– CHOWDAYYA OF THE FERRYMEN

If what they say is true, I'm practising
the art of the breathing dummy: impermanent,
hovering between realms of yesterday,
then, now, tomorrow, later.

Later never comes the way you expect it to;
darkly red or sun-kissed or crimson.
Instead, a pale egg-white wash
of realization. Something you knew

all along but refused to believe,
lying like a gall stone in the wall of tummy.
Later is the air settling like tired dust
in the plains of our arteries and veins,

discolouring the skies, petrifying the earth,
telling us it's too heavy to walk through here.
It's the old Kurdish woman, standing
on her balcony off Edgware Road

in her green caftan, clouds emerging
from her head, looking to the streets below
for a man – not her husband – who gave her
a scarf that burned like his skin once

before vanishing somewhere deep –
a jungle or valley, some place of war,
where she lost the patterns, the touch,
the smooth complexity of him.

The Day after the Death of My Imaginary Child

Is a moment in the doorway
of an underground cave
with paintings of bright buffalo,
pinpricks of rain.
It's when the spider of dream
that's been shadowing me
since I bled my way to womanhood
whispers again,
how I'll outlive any child
I could hope to bear,
for thinking that a body
made of sand and water
could dare to make one of silver.

The day after the death
of my imaginary child
is a day I count separately
like a resolute wave
spewing up finger-pink
birthmarks, tips of brooding,
foamy hair. It's knowing

that at the end
there'll be the same brush
of swallow, spit, sudden light.
I'll be asked to spend myself
over molecule of son or daughter –
take all that failed infinity
of body, fibre, blood
and surrender it as harvest
to the seasons of the famished sea.

The Floral Carpet

Prelude

I am tired of walking in darkness.
It is not of being swallowed
that I am afraid.

What is the sound of love?
What is fuck? What is *I would like to sleep with you?*
What is *Why have you wet your bed again?*

Because the dark comes with the sound of cats mating.

You asked me why.

Because I pray every night

And God doesn't come with the dark or with the sound of cats mating.

Ode to the Moon

(On the way to Perkins Diner – Cleveland, Ohio)

Oh luminous sun sitting whole and bright,
sitting pretty
like the love I left behind in San Francisco.
Oh lost love, mooning lover, plump porker.

Inside the Comfort Inn

(also Cleveland, Ohio)

He cannot peel the skin off me
or touch my breasts with his beard.
He cannot, in fact, reach me at all.

His face up my shirt,
his roving hands,
his chin, the scratching hairs.

Can I leave now? Please can I go?

All this is old.
Older than my imagination.

A naked lady in the tub
scrubbing the insides of her thighs,
unravelled hair around her shoulders.

The hotel soap, a tiny rectangle
in the heart of her hand
scrubbing the insides, all the insides.

Saying, *Why, oh why is this me?*

When she runs, the backs of her slippers – how they run with her, beating stems, destroying petals, peeling the *what are they called?*
Those skeins, delicate life-giving strings, chlorophyll-holding green skeins.
Even the poor veinlets, the calyxes, the drooping stamen and drifting pollen –
All in the whirlwind of her slippers.
The roots, the very roots, she could dissolve, she thinks, there is enough rug, enough fur, enough to encase herself – to lie in wait for his footsteps.

London

Waking beside a broad and empty face
I lie to him about what moves me.
And it is nothing to do with wooden farmhouses,
cathedrals, or damp grass.

It is nothing to do with what brought me to him,
or the perpetual blue sky I've given up
to be here in Rathbone Place,
his bed of white, ragged spaces.

That lifeless life, the thick body he carries around
under his skin – what have these to do
with meeting in the middle of listless winter
full of drink and desperateness?

I pick up my uncleanliness, six black pieces
of clothing and slip into the morning.
London at 7 a.m. is grey, unmoving –
a city in slow recovery.

It is only ache after all that takes us anywhere –
so I return, to a borrowed room,
a collection of things resembling
nothing and stubbornly strange to me.

All night there has been such heaving.
The wind outside is full of noise, raging.
But it is quiet here, by myself, alone,
with ideas of love and not much else.

London II

How good it is to wake up with you, he says.
I've been awake for hours now
hearing him snore with a wind in his throat
of wine and cigarettes from the night before.

He's not *that* old, I keep telling myself.
Ten years younger than my father, and younger
in the hard lines of his body that cleaves
itself to mine like Kathleen Ferrier's voice

playing on his record from another age –
so haunting and strong it makes me want to leave,
go to where his smell is not on me,
or this cold morning's clamour

for a memory of waking in half-light –
the ancient fan click-clicking in turns,
the only harshness coming from the morning crow
reminding us to raise our soft, eager bodies,

to begin the drive down the city's forsaken streets,
past pavement dwellers and the saw-toothed ocean.
Reaching my parent's gates – the locked iron bars
like a field of giant mallows – I clamber over,

and creep quietly into my own cotton sheets,
clutching to a love too young to breathe.

Homecoming

I forgot how Madras loves noise –
loves neighbours and pregnant women
and gods and babies

and Brahmins who rise
like fire hymns to sear the air
with habitual earthquakes.

How funeral processions clatter
down streets with drums and rose petals,
dancing death into deafness.

How vendors and cats make noises
of love on bedroom walls and alleyways
of night, operatic and dark.

How cars in reverse sing 'Jingle Bells'
and scooters have larynxes of lorries.
How even colour can never be quiet.

How fisherwomen in screaming red –
with skirts and incandescent third eyes
and bangles like rasping planets

and Tamil women on their morning walks
in saris and jasmine and trainers
can shred the day and all its skinny silences.

I forgot how a man dying under the body
of a tattered boat could ask for promises;
how they could be as soundless as the sea

on a wounded day, altering the ground
of the earth as simply as the sun filtering through –
the monsoon rain dividing everything.

Overnight in the Dance Theatre

I have visited in my wanderings, shrines and other places of pilgrimage, but I have not seen another shrine, blissful like my body. – SARAHA

I am waiting among the bakul trees
for a line of the moon to catch the stones
at my throat, for the goddess to appear
with starlit palms at the doorway to save me.

Instead, a girl I passed a month ago
in Thiruvanthapura, is here on the steps
in striped panties, eating mangosteens,
tossing bruised and purple skins at my feet.

Your body is your universe, she sighs,
prising open hearts of things in her hands:
water, spirit, sand, till everything's held –
even bodies raw from dereliction,
mending themselves again, as the muted lisp
of morning's tongue pushes against the sky.

On the Burning of an Unfamiliar Aunt

My family gathers around to mourn,
but mainly to whisper
how killing yourself
amounts to confessing
Life somehow got too much for you.

Something Camus figured out
between the war years in Algeria
and the car crash in Yonne –
in the hip, smoky days
of tuberculosis and love.

We're tracing a journey back
to the nebula of our aunt's heart,
to frayed white diamonds
and a forest of fireflies.
Our aunt shouts from the space

between this absurdity and the next.
It's the shape of oblivion she sees –
and it's a simple thing – a line
as graceful as a leg once might have been,
burning like a giant red star

in the slow hurl towards its own death,
leaving cores of crystal breath
on the windows of childhood.
The body's been burning,
innocent of its fires. All its life

the body's been burning,
our aunt says, running from brightness,
greedy for air, scurrying like a man.
to his mother's feet
to this single realization.

Something Camus must have done
as the Facel Vega danced stupidly
into the plane tree, the delicate
French rain diffusing his final words
as though they were his first.

And when the whimper of flame
struggled to release itself
from the relic of his broken throat –
he might have held it there for a while,
like a secret; like the mutiny of abiding sleep.

On Becoming a Dancer

I saw a man immerse himself today.
And how he did it – sliding
into a green surface of water and lily pads,

a flimsy piece of cloth wrapped around his bones –
his bottom – bare and brown and taut,
lowering like light into glass.

Outside, all that was living was making up a life
for itself – the deep mud tracks, the rocks
and pink houses, the bullocks chained together,

the women with shaven heads slipping
across the road. And the men in the lorry
in front of us, pointing and smirking,

saying something lewd, their words
reaching through the glass to touch me
in a hollow, incomplete way.

So when I'm home, lying vanquished
in my own bed, searching for what is slow
and lonely, I pare my knees apart, point my toes.

At the Rodin Museum

Rilke is following me everywhere
with his tailor-made suits
and vegetarian smile.

He says because I'm young,
I'm always beginning,
and cannot know love.

He sees how I'm a giant piece
of glass again, trying
to catch the sun

in remote corners of rooms,
mountain tops, uncertain
places of light.

He speaks of the cruelty
of hospitals, the stillness
of cathedrals,

takes me through bodies
and arms and legs
of such extravagant size,

the ancient sky burrows in
with all the dead words
we carry and cannot use.

He holds up mirrors
from which our reflections fall –
half-battered existences,

where we lose ourselves
for the sake of the other,
and the others still to come.

The Kandy Museum, Sri Lanka

Here, among brocade jackets of Sinhala kings
and demon masks of Mahasohonyaka,
I finally understand the idea of entanglement.

How it's possible that you can watch with me,
the fish-tailed women with creepers
for arms arcing into primeval time,

holding lotus flowers in bloom and ola books
with secrets for snakebites – the pages bound
like pieces of our absent skin.

In Physics, it's called the state of interaction:
two particles coming in contact with each other,
as I think we did, bound thereafter in space and time.

Making it so the ravines of your muddy eyes
stretch to where I stand on moonstone steps
with misshapen elephants and lions,

just as our night of discovery lives suspended
between your summer of stars and spiders,
and my winter, tropically sad.

It means events fall through:
a universe can oppose itself,
spill down the walls of its own making;

that even your wife, finding her way
between Buddha's tooth and 195 dead Britishers,
must hunt for treasures in the dust like the rest of us.

And as she lifts you by the tired shirtsleeves
to the house in the burning bush
where the children are waiting,

you're still leaning against the garage door
saying how rain feels like sin,
feeding our moments to the bodies of winds.

Aftermath

So we are left to count up the gods
before our charge of mining. To enter
the deeper earth of origins, birthings

There are lines between us –
subterranean pillars of inconsistency.
So when you speak of *emptiness, light,*

reality; colours of the prism
borne on the hypotenuse, the radius,
the corrugated boundaries of myth,

you see me lumbered with all this talk
of single things being multiplied
as they pass through surfaces of fear.

Say the horizons are suddenly awash;
awash and floating away on staggered knees.
Say we understand how weight only gives

at a single, inaccessible point.
How *shambles* can mean a way of walking
or the description of a messy scene.

Say the gods, so used to divining,
would reach out from their abodes
and risk our imaginations.

Say *ocean* as the deep breathing place
of colourless centres. Say it,
so we can find our place.

The Fasting Season

The rains have arrived
and my three aunts
grown maritally large
like watermelons
will starve and warm
themselves with prayers;
refuse water, food, spit,
and sex – imagine their bodies
as they were before.

For eight days they'll follow
these patterns of thinning
and clearing. *Indulgence*
is violence, they'll say –
the big fat words of deprivation
fleeing their arid lips
till every hungry filament
of desire is drowned
in a blight of devotion.

At sunset I take mango stones
for their throats so they can break
fast with the still wet roads,
gather exigencies of great light
like their adored saint
Gosala, who sent his soul
raring through the river-
length of his spine
like dust into the world.

Love in Carlisle

Girls were crying yesterday in their ball gowns;
holding each other up like poles of wilted beanstalks.
I wanted to carry them into the streets.
To the unused railroad track in the middle of town,
unwrap the past and lay before them
a fragile girl I once knew, walking towards love
in a thin, determined way. That she should live here too –
in this town of carefully-guarded houses
and old ladies in rocking chairs
in fake pearls and printed button-down dresses.

Girls are crying in their ball gowns and boys
are holding them up and taking them to the streets,
to warehouses or backs of deserted pick-up trucks.
A troubadour waits on a wooden porch
for the faultless girl, to speak her name,
undress her, give noise to her that is new and violent.
The old ladies form a line and hold photographs
against their faces where the skin used to be unbroken.
They step out from their dresses and kick off their shoes,
cross over the barren tracks in their solitary dance.

Pangs for the Philanderer

I miss you – your glittering life
and marcasite eyes.
Where I am now, it is all made of nylon;
smelling of talcum powder and envy,
maudlin curtains and stockings,
serrated bed covers,
rooms denuded from pleasure.

The day softens.
The whole day, now that I hold
it up in the cracked light
of the windows, is legendary
and alone, making its way in haste
to the scene by the water.

If I remove one of the pieces
where the shoreline of her face
is unfolding like crimson branches;
the green swimsuit glowing –
evanescent and sylvan –
you might still be here:
distant, unattainable.

Open Hands

In Nairobi, an albino boy followed me everywhere
peering at me from behind cupboards and trees,
chortling with glee: *Hello, fine!*
Here is space. Here is space.

It is open and large and dark here
and I feel open and large and dark.

I'm moving into a scene already imagined,
a life already waiting under the topaz sky,
under the blue lacquered trees where the dust
is spiralling up to hide it.

The boy teaches me names of animals.
They are spread out and running under us:
giraffe, lion, hippopotamus – *twiga, simba, kiboko.*

What if it isn't true that we inherit our homes?
It's lovely here isn't, the boy says.
It's lovely.

So we must make meanings of things:
a carcass of a jackal in a baobab tree,
a man's fingers pushing up the straps of your maroon dress,
a low wood-beamed room full of misgivings.

The boy holds me in his lanolin arms,
looks at me as though I were a sheet of glass,
a single antelope facing a row of acacias,
an unending ruinous landscape.

It's the hardest thing to do –
to take him aside, feel his pigmentless skin –
explain how there's so much space
I've lost myself.

How I cannot be this woman
looking to a foreign sky for the day,
disappeared again, leaving only a dim glow
in my hands to remember it by.

In the House of the Abandoned Portuguese Hillside

A boy cuts out a piece of sky,
runs through the rubble dusting off stones,
half-made walls, the solitary window.

A handsome dark-haired boy.

When he's done, he folds up the sky
and hangs it where the ceiling should have been
to guard the village in the valley.

It is a house with no histories.
Without pictures in pewter frames or grandfather clocks.
It is a house without.

When he leaves, the sky lets out a wail,
cries through its skin. The house chimes along;
fills the hillside with lonesome wind, longing.

A woman wanders in from where the orange trees grow,
sits at the window with a closed-up face
and black-rimmed eyes.

In the afternoon light, austere and even,
she thinks about what she'll do to fill up
the holes within her.

The house coats her, nudges her
towards the village in the valley;
puts diamond pins in her eyes.

She's still sitting there when the boy returns.
The handsome dark-haired boy.

He's watching her against the broken frames,
the sky turning purple in her arms,
its tail wrapped around her waist.

It's the same anguished purple of deep holes,
the melodramatic purple of love burgeoning,
then dying. Purple smoke from the stoves

of the Portuguese houses down there –
in the village where whole families call
to wives and mothers, sit at tables, wait for supper.

He stands for hours, watching her like a painting;
how the sky takes her diamond pins for stars,
leaves her like a whisper and falls into the valley.

He could bring her some warm slippers, he thinks;
a knitted shawl. He could touch the angle of her face
where everything seems to begin.

He could lie at her feet until she decided to sleep.

Bamboo Man

He came to me again last night.
Look into me, he demanded. Of course it was a trick.
I picked him up meaning to be gentle;
removing his layers, my fingers twitching,
leaping for his collar, wondering how it would be
to have something whole in my palms.
After every fibre had been peeled, his voice came back.
Fool, fool. Bamboos have no hearts. Bamboos are hollow.
Then the pieces came together.
He was a man again, and he left.

When he comes now, I wait with hammers.
This has gone on long enough, I say.
I want my dream of the giant snow leopard back.
Remember? With the transparent pool and the ochre forest.
When I am held by him and not afraid?
And the bamboo man says, *Oh yes, and that wonderful part*
about the silver. He smirks.
I don't care, don't you know?
Then I plead with my collected tears.
Anything, I whisper. *Anything, even the dream of the fallen teeth,*
where I kill my family. Even the dead dog,
illegitimate child, my father by the broken swings
asking if he's worth anything, the bottle-bombs around us.

I know you have them in your pockets, I scream.
and then back to whispering – *Or nothing then, give me nothing.*

One day I force myself to think only of the soul
I will find for the bamboo man. Before I sleep, it is there –
a magical thread twined around my fingers.
I practise the loop to trap his tiny waist.
The soul has been instructed well: grow thick, rise
mountain-like, melt, overflow into his mouth.
When the heavy drops fall, he's skidding around in surprise;
his movements jerky and unmeasured.
Then it is all a dissolved mess – a floating coat
in shattered sound. I spend the night sorting
through the gore – green fibres coming apart
in my hands – knee-deep in ripples and waves.
The sides of the picture get smaller, I am running out of time.
I do not leave till I find the gentle, beating thing –
a gift for his empty pockets.

Hill Travel

Eucalyptus have been travelling for years,
lascivious for Indian earth – watery roots
and canopied heads like lashings
of liquorice in these hills.

Australian missionaries, wistful, I imagine,
planted them among the sholar and neem.
The Vicar's wife scaling steps
with saplings against her chest,

thinking it would do the natives good
to look upwards, stand at the feet of God.

The year my parents ran away to be alone,
our oldest one lay across the driveway,
its 100-foot body abandoned
in its own bed of leaves.

The rain, unforgiving, shimmying down
the piebald length of it, kissed its body
as my parents must have done
in that first mist of morning,

thinking of ways to dispense – the torso,
damaged limbs, emasculated soil.

They took pictures, sightless conquerors.
My mother like a goddess, her many arms
twirling around in frenzy,
her foot in the carcass's throat.

My father, by the rhododendron bush,
watching the light fall in grave silences
through the camera's unbending eye,
touching the stringy root of it.

How simple really, to begin eternity,
to call the things of the ground your own.

AJ, Age 15

I once chased my brother
down to the edge of the sea.
We ran past sheets and towels
spread like sky on the beach,
between strips of cloth,
drying chilli and tamarind.
Past slums shackled to the shore –
a maze of thatch roofs and cowdung
caked walls. And then I lost him,
searched loudly for him, called his name.
Said, *Come out or else* –
all the usual tricks.

A woman cleaning rice on her knees
in a blouse done up with safety pins
pointed to a hut with a single weary finger –
where he was hiding with a water buffalo.
The low blue lights of the television flickering.
He was inside, laughing so hard,
shaking his head back and forth,
I thought the joy would come tearing out from him.
Afterwards, we sat in something like silence –
his rare chubby hand in mine,
listening to the breath of living water.

AJ Turns 27

My brother sits in a room
of broken limbs and broken minds,
sifting through the myriad parts
to mend the fracture in his heart.
If he would slide across the floor
to the boy whose legs are lessons
in fragility and swop a joint of knee
for a chromosome,
or barter one cauliflower ear
with the deaf and dumb lad
in the corner wrapping streamers
around his body as if it were a river –
he could maybe find a space
to dive into the water's depth,
to rustle up these myrmidons –
these rags of boys against the window light –
and lead them from this mansion
of existences to carrion fields
with barren backs and virgin clavicles.
He could soften the hollows
of their simple necks, and it would be
a joyous thing to see my brother sorting still –
a king among these human wrecks.

Leakages

He finds himself against a wall again,
dying to break through the surface, loosen
himself like cracks of monsoon rain.

He must stand or crouch, knees apart,
a fortified satellite of lights and senses.
These are the fingers he uses to touch.

He's spreading an invasion of locusts
like tears against a face he helped make once
in a room of bathrobes and roses.

There was leaning then: an afternoon
of murky dusks; a copper gathering of limb
and hair collected in his chest.

He comes back to himself, drop by drop,
leaves behind garbled pieces to gratify
the earth – the knowing dregs.

Now it's over, he can wipe the sweat,
the million bony beads of lust, the quietness.
He can pick up his trousers, fasten them.

Back home there's a woman who waits.
Moves from basin to drain; buttons shirts;
remedies ruins, taints, hurts.

He walks over to this memory of wife,
tells her it's over. He's emptied of it. See –
it lies in a flaccid pit of sleep, blurred.

The Last Class

Here, on this patch of lawn, it is over.
I watch you smooth your shirt as you leave,
gathering your books. When you look at me,
that awkward light in your eyes from the sun,
I want to tell you what we mean –
that underneath, there is a sadness

we know nothing about. A sadness
pushing through the day like rain, over-
whelming everything; that the day, in a mean
attempt to hold us in its fingers and leaves
has failed. You turn colours in the sun;
fade into an injured green behind me.

What I want to say is this: *Come to me.*
Stay. Do something about this sadness.
Everything old can be broken for reasons.
It is quiet and the sun is moving over
the shadow of sky like these Baltimore leaves:
fallen, streaked, orange, mean.

I walk home with a song of a meaning
singing its throaty blue way to me
while this August day and its loosening leaves
slips by bearing its own sadness.
The house painters working over
at the neighbours are resting in the sun.

They're reading papers in the sun
in overalls and grizzly chests and meaningful
silences. Their bodies, like boats, drifting over
the same horizon where you are watching me
stare at their paint-stained knees, their sadness
dancing out of the radio, unmoored in a heap of leaves.

When I turn to face you, you are leavened
against the tops of row houses, gleaming in the sun.
You've come to explain about the sadness,
to follow me down the basement stairs. Meaning,
of course, to salvage the day between you and me,
to say what remains can never be over.

But what I see is a leaf in the sun, a painter beckoning me.
It is sadness after all, carried over the neighbour's fence.
It seems to say, *This is a day. This is everything it could mean.*

The Opening up of the Sun

First there was the sun
then the opening up of the sun
then the sun screaming
then September

My brother is losing his mind
We watch him
We wear name-tags on our chests
He cannot read but we must do something
to make him recognize us

We revive everything he has ever loved
My father comes home and watches *Tom and Jerry* cartoons
My mother lies in bed singing nursery rhymes
She strokes his forehead and says *My poor poor baby*
My sister and I build entire Fisher-Price villages

We take him back to the cottage
We get there by train
We ask him *Do you want to go?*
Do you want?
We watch him sit on the wall vacant
facing the cottage
sun streaming into his back

The opening up of the sun involves
skimming splinters stretching satiation

For weeks he walks around looking for his comb
Comb has been dead for years now

At the swimming pool he jumps in and out in and out
In the bath he soaps himself
squeezes the sponge between his toes
between his legs like he's been taught to do

He was born in August
A Sunday in August

Scream: utter piercing cry

He was a child who never cried
Now they say he's depressed
He spends days in the room
breaking up villages and sobbing
We build them back again and sob with him

It is September
My brother is going to die
He falls through the gap in our family laughing

He stitches up the seams in the sun
He takes September
like his pink plastic comb
and rests it on his chest
while underneath his damaged heart
stills and starts stills and starts

Love Poem in Haste

In you, a single blue country
laid bare of inconsistencies.
A bone of truth caught in a cage of fire.

When you speak,
it is dust rising from the throat,
circus lights on a blackened river.

There are spaces between us
faint as churchyards in June,
sweetening our mud-filled bodies.

And there is the ocean –
gathering itself,
telling us what we are not.

Turning into Men Again

This morning men are returning to the world,
waiting on the sides of blackened pavements
for a rickshaw to carry them away
on the sharp pins and soles of their dancing feet.

They must go to the houses of their childhoods
to be soothed. They must wait for the wheels
to appear from the thin arm of road.
They must catch the crack in the sky

where the light shifts from light to dark
to light again, like the body in the first stages of love;
angering, heightening, spreading:
bent knees, bent breath.

Now they are moving, changing colours.
Women are standing at the thresholds of doors,
holding jars of oil, buckets of hot water and salt,
calamine, crushed mint and drink.

Some crawl into their mother's laps,
collapse against the heavy bosoms of old nannies,
search for the girl who climbed with them
to the tin roof for the first time.

Inside, in the shadows of pillars,
fathers and grandfathers are stepping down
from picture frames with secrets on their lips,
calling the lost in from their voyages.

Countries of the Body

For the way the moon rose in the sky last night, my love –
orange and eerie like a scene from a parallel life
where we are married with children of our own
and your wife is the lady with the crimson dress
with ruffles down her breasts, sleeping in a country
of dreams while we dance through a room of strangers.

She's the stranger in the park, the stranger
who follows me home, taking apart the loveless
night. She sees me waver from country to country,
adjusting the curtains so no one can see this life
where the sky moves in and out of the world, dressed
like a starlet in stockings on streets of her own.

Here are the adulterers playing games of their own:
husbands and wives by river banks, unmasking strangers
as in the movies where one body undresses
the other, strips it bare like a blue gum tree, loves
with markings, territories; disconnects life
so it's impossible to put back the countries

where they used to belong. These bodies of countries –
they are our tracks of line and dirt, our own
set of timeless days in the park. They play out. A life
always plays out with somebody watching. The stranger
in the shadows spying while a man and woman make love.
See, the fingers move up the seam of crimson dress,

part, like bruised wings of a butterfly. And the dress –
shorn of its layers – lies like the ruin of a country
in such despair it cannot name the names for love.
Your wife steps in, pulls the dress over her hips, her own
discs of bone and flesh. *Where've you been to, stranger?*
the dress mutters, as it slides under the floor of my life –

cracks the thing apart, hinges on your wife; her life
swimming back into the sky as the moon dresses
the night in orange. See how light falls, licks at the stranger;
how two women will lead each other out of a country
to sort out wombs, scars, faces. Exchange the others for her own –
pull two ends of a curtain open, empty out the rooms of love.

Suicide, Early January

Before she leaves,
she imagines him –
a cathedral in the sky,
soaking and soaking her
to the skin.

He's at the window,
balanced like a diver
off the sliver
of English winter light,
holding keys

to a yellowing
childhood Delhi house.
Your love is like a drowning,
she wants to say,
to the rose-glass lips

staining the dark
estuary of day. *So tell me,*
love – the words unfolding,
like petals of desire
between her eyes,

How is it I'm still bone dry?
He'll fumble then,
with curtains of despair,
rush to fill the gaps
of her disenchantment.

Is this how I must be saved?
she'll ask, through pigeons,
in the loquat trees,
salt and dust,
desert silences.

Like this, he'll answer,
sweeping the rain
of her never-cut hair
into the hollows of his blood,
birthing her again

in the burnished rust
of the future, gloaming –
a teardrop raked
against the small broken
moment of her beginning.

Familiar Shores

I am miles from home, in Mombassa,
putting diamonds in my ears
like a woman with three names
instead of one.

And there she is again, my mother,
walking through the French doors
towards the Indian Ocean
because she cannot bear to see me.

At night, I turn into a body I do not know.
He turns me into a stream,
a river falling over a cliff.
A word from him that doesn't come –

and I am on my knees, backed up
against a wall, under the table
resting against his thigh, asking
for things I didn't think I could want.

My mother is straining against the sea;
its malicious blue face and white streamers

wrapping her body, pushing it down
to the bottomless dark.

When she resurfaces on a new beach,
she doesn't speak for days.
She sees me place one foot
into ginger silk panties,

and then dance and dance
from this bleached body
to the next – an island in search
of her own familiar shores.

Sunrise at Sanchi Stupa

after W.S. Merwin

O fire, thou art the son of heaven by the body of earth.
– Rig Veda

We were sitting outside the stupa
that morning when the sun shone down
like a woman sweeping clear roads of dust
and dreams making me wonder if love
can find its way like this through broken
valleys past shattered edge of bramble
thorn and bruised foundation of monastery
all-conquering love doesn't stir
in the dark to talk to guards doesn't have
the quietness of cows doesn't run with incensed rage
across the bougainvillea fringe of the world
If love were really born of fire we'd build
giant domes of sky around our gossiping pasts
and silence them with bits of tooth or graft
of hoary nail we'd let the road consume
our steps our columns of desire
and when morning broke the scattering earth
with blood red points of light all the distances
of night would brush us by as the undergrowth
of our unfinished lives

ACKNOWLEDGEMENTS

Grateful acknowledgement to the editors of the following magazines in which these poems first appeared, sometimes in earlier versions: *The Times Literary Supplement*: 'London'; *The Southern Poetry Review*: 'Bamboo Man,' 'The Deliverer'; *Reactions 4* (Pen & Inc Press): 'Familiar Shores,' 'Later,' 'Love in Carlisle 3,' 'In the House of the Abandoned Portuguese Hillside,' 'The Affair II,' 'Turning into Men Again,' 'London II,' 'Undertow'; *Wasafiri*: 'Overnight in the Dance Theatre,' 'At the Rodin Museum,' 'On the Burning of an Unfamiliar Aunt,' 'Homecoming'; *Atlas*: 'Countries of the Body,' 'On Becoming a Dancer,' 'The Affair'.

'Why language? They
ask, why not medicine
or magic? Why not
something more useful?'
(Kala Krishnan Ramesh)

The editors at HarperCollins believe that poetry is medicine, magic and more. Committed to publishing the most exciting contemporary poetry from India and the subcontinent, we wanted to celebrate ten of our favourite books by publishing them as special keepsake editions under the 'Poetry 10' series. From sci-fi verse to modern bhakti poetry, long narrative sequences about birth and identity to brief sonnets, each book will speak to lovers (and haters) of poetry with wit, wisdom, clarity and abandon.

3 Sections by Vijay Seshadri
All One's Blue by Kazim Ali
Bearings by Karthika Naïr
Countries of the Body by Tishani Doshi
He Is Honey, Salt and the Most Perfect Grammar by Kala Krishnan Ramesh
Life & Times of Mr S by Vivek Narayanan
Malabar Mind by Anita Nair
Space Gulliver: Chronicles of an Alien by Sampurna Chattarji
Triage: Casualties of Love and Sex by Margaret Mascarenhas
When God Is a Traveller by Arundhathi Subramaniam

Tishani Doshi's debut collection, *Countries of the Body*, marks the arrival of a major new voice in international poetry. Winner of the 2006 Forward Poetry Prize for best first collection, each poem in the book sings of the body with all its contours and contradictions, failures and flaws. Attuned to the precision of dance, the rhythm of these lines can tell 'movement from half-movement'. Shuttling between ancient ruins, sea towns and inhabiting the mysterious spaces between dream and memory, the poems will enchant readers with their delicate and haunting quality.